# My Little Book of
# Weather

by Claudia Martin

Publisher: Maxime Boucknooghe
Editorial Director: Victoria Garrard
Art Director: Miranda Snow
Project Editor: Joanna McInerney
Design and editorial: Tall Tree Ltd

First published in the UK in 2016 by
QED Publishing
Part of The Quarto Group
The Old Brewery
6 Blundell Street
London N7 9BH

www.qed-publishing.co.uk

A catalogue record for this book is available from the British Library

ISBN 978 1 78493 453 8

Printed in China

Words in **bold** are explained in the glossary on page 60.

# Contents

# What is weather?

The **weather** can be rainy or snowy, sunny or cloudy, hot or cold, windy or calm.

At this moment, the weather is different all over the world. In some places, rain is pouring down. In other places, it has not rained for months.

« A rainbow forms when sunlight passes through drops of rain.

>> Antarctica is the world's coldest place. The temperature can drop to a very chilly -93° Celsius.

<< One of the world's hottest places is Dallol in Ethiopia, Africa. Temperatures can reach about 46° Celsius.

5

# Our atmosphere

The Earth is surrounded by a blanket of **air**. This is called the **atmosphere**.

>> As you travel up through the atmosphere, the air gets thinner and the temperature gets colder.

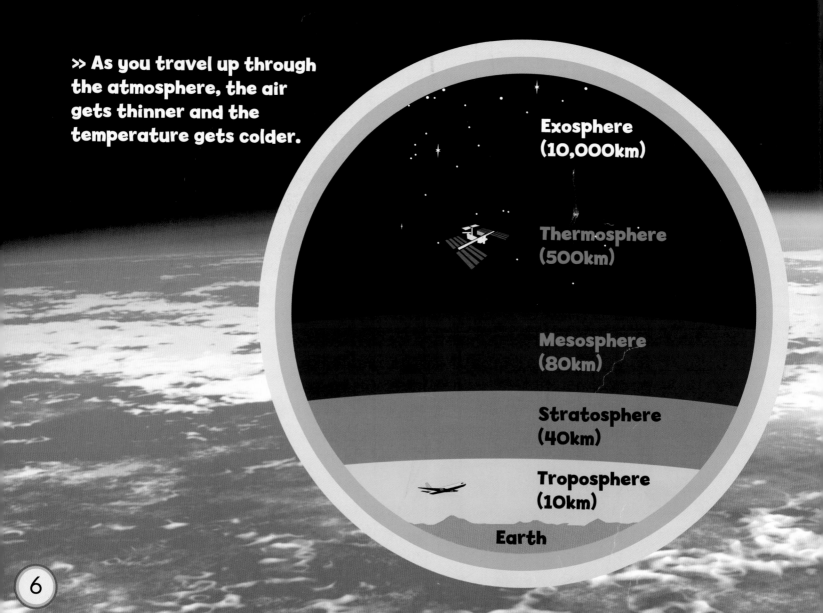

Exosphere
(10,000km)

Thermosphere
(500km)

Mesosphere
(80km)

Stratosphere
(40km)

Troposphere
(10km)

Earth

All our weather happens in the layer of the atmosphere closest to the Earth. This is where droplets of water form clouds and where swirling air creates wind.

>> The atmosphere contains the air that humans, animals and plants need to survive.

<< The atmosphere can be seen from space. It looks like a blue haze, with a low layer of clouds.

# Warmed by the Sun

Weather is caused by the Sun warming the Earth and its atmosphere. The atmosphere keeps the Earth warm by trapping the Sun's heat, like a blanket.

Because the Earth is shaped like a ball, the Sun does not heat everywhere on the surface the same amount. It heats areas closer to the **Equator** much more than it heats the **poles**.

⌄ At the Equator, the Sun's rays hit the Earth straight on, making temperatures there very hot.

North Pole

Equator

South Pole

« At the poles, the Sun's rays hit the Earth at an angle, so temperatures there remain very low.

9

# Why the wind blows

What causes howling winds and gentle breezes? It all starts when air is warmed by the Sun, making it expand and rise.

« Winds are named after the direction they are blowing from. A southerly wind blows from the south.

When warm air rises, cooler air rushes in to fill its place. We feel that movement as wind. Warm, rising air creates **low pressure**, because it is not pressing down hard on the Earth. Cool, sinking air creates high pressure.

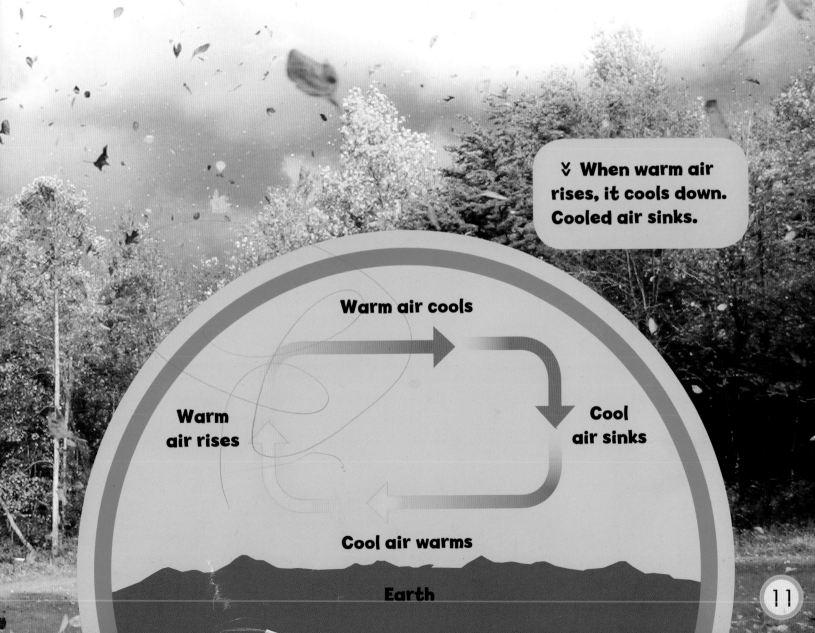

⋎ When warm air rises, it cools down. Cooled air sinks.

Warm air cools

Warm air rises

Cool air sinks

Cool air warms

Earth

# Water on the move

When the Sun heats oceans and lakes, a little water **evaporates**. This water turns into an invisible gas called **water vapour**.

Clouds

Evaporation

>>The Water Cycle

Ocean

Stream

« When water droplets in a cloud get too big and heavy, they fall to the ground as rain.

Warm air can hold a lot of water vapour. But when warm air rises and cools, it cannot hold so much. Some of the water **condenses** back into droplets of water, forming clouds.

**Rain**

**Snow**

**Evaporation**

**Rivers and lakes**

# Climate

The type of weather that you can expect in an area over the course of a year is called **climate**.

‍⌄ **Areas with a** tropical **rainforest climate are near the Equator. These areas are hot and rainy all year.**

« **North America and much of Europe have a** temperate **climate. Summers are not too hot, and winters are not too cold.**

The climate of an area depends on how close it is to the Equator, how near it is to the sea, and how high it is. An area's climate affects what plants and animals can live there.

>> High mountains have a cold and windy climate.

# The seasons

In most places, the weather changes through the year, creating seasons. Each season has a different pattern of weather.

**⌄ Temperate areas of the world have four seasons: spring, summer, autumn and winter.**

**Spring**                    **Summer**

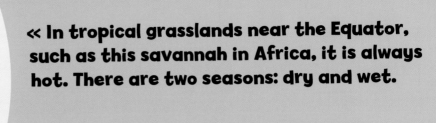

« In tropical grasslands near the Equator, such as this savannah in Africa, it is always hot. There are two seasons: dry and wet.

We have seasons because the Earth is tilted as it travels around the Sun. The half of the Earth tilted towards the Sun has summer, while the half tilted away has winter.

Autumn

Winter

# Climate change

The Earth is getting warmer.
This is making its climates change.
Humans help cause the changes by
not taking enough care of the planet.

« **Hot and dry places
are getting even hotter,
drier and dustier.**

Cars and factories
release a gas called
carbon dioxide.
This gas traps extra
heat in the atmosphere,
making the Earth slowly
warm up. This is called
global warming.

⌄ A coal factory in China
is puffing carbon dioxide
into the atmosphere.

⌄ As the Earth gets warmer, the
extra heat in the atmosphere
causes more extreme weather,
such as storms and floods.

# Clouds

Clouds are masses of water droplets or **ice crystals**. If you look at the clouds you will find clues about what the weather will do.

^ Cirrus clouds are thin, wispy and high. They contain ice crystals. They do not produce rain.

There is always water in the air, floating as invisible water vapour. When the air cools or gets too full of water vapour, a cloud of water droplets forms. If the air is very cold, the water freezes into ice crystals.

⌃ Stratus clouds are low and grey. They form when warm air blows over cold air. They bring rain or snow.

« Cumulus clouds form when warm air rises. They are white and puffy. If they stay white, it will not rain.

# Fog

Fog and mist are clouds that form near the ground. Mist is a light fog.

« Fog and mist can also form when warm air rises over a mountain, making it cool and form droplets.

On a winter night, fog can appear when air close to the ground cools and forms water droplets. Fog often happens near the sea, where the air is full of water vapour.

⌄ Thick fog stops you seeing more than a few metres. Drivers and aircraft pilots must take extra care.

⌃ Mist is when the air is not clear, but you can see for up to 1 kilometre.

# Rain

When a cloud looks grey, it is probably about to rain. Its droplets or ice crystals are joining together and getting big enough to fall.

˅ **A quick rain shower can happen when damp air rises on a warm day.**

Apart from in hot, tropical areas, most raindrops start as ice crystals. They melt as they fall. Tiny drops are called drizzle. When a mass of warm air is blown over cold air, we get heavy, long-lasting rain.

« Umbrellas help to keep us dry during a rain shower.

>> Cherrapunjee in India is one of the world's wettest places. It gets 9.5 metres of rain a year.

# Snow

Snowflakes form when ice crystals in a cloud stick together. When they get heavy enough, they start to fall.

⌄ Snow will settle if the temperature on the ground is below freezing: 0° Celsius.

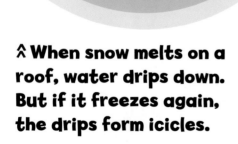

⌃ When snow melts on a roof, water drips down. But if it freezes again, the drips form icicles.

Snow can only reach the ground when the temperature of the air is below 2° Celsius. If it is warmer, the flakes will melt in the air.

⩔ **Snowflakes form in many different shapes. They usually have six sides or points but are not perfectly** symmetrical.

# Frost

Have you ever woken up to see a sparkling coating of ice on the ground, plants, cars or windows? That is frost.

⌄ Rime frost can be very thick. It is made when water droplets in fog freeze onto objects.

>> When water vapour freezes onto plants, tiny ice crystals are formed. This is called hoar frost.

Frost usually appears overnight, in winter. Frost is caused by water vapour or droplets freezing onto cold surfaces.

⌄ Frost can form inside windows. This is called fern frost because the ice crystals make leaf shapes.

# Thunderstorms

Thunderclouds can form when hot, damp air rises at the end of a warm day. Inside these towering clouds, ice crystals swirl about.

⌄ **Thunderclouds are wider at the top than at the bottom. They are called cumulonimbus.**

As the ice crystals brush each other, they make **static electricity**. The electricity builds up until a spark of lightning is created. The spark sets off **shockwaves** in the air. We hear these as thunder.

⌄ **When lightning sparks from one part of a cloud to another, it can light up the sky. This is sheet lightning.**

« **A branching spark of static electricity is jumping from a cloud to the ground. This is called fork lightning.**

# Hail

Hailstones can weigh up to 1 kilogram – as much as a pineapple. Luckily, most hailstones are much smaller.

Hailstones are lumps of ice that form inside thunderclouds. Ice crystals in the clouds are hurled about until they join into lumps. They can fall at 160 kilometres per hour.

« A storm of heavy hailstones smashed this car windscreen.

<< The Great Plains of the United States are known as Hail Alley. They get up to nine days of hail a year.

>> This record-breaking hailstone fell in South Dakota, USA, in 2010. It is 20 centimetres wide.

# Gales

When the wind is moving faster than 62 kilometres per hour, it's time to take shelter! You're in a gale.

Gales are common during winter in cooler areas of North America and Europe. They are caused by violent movements of hot and cold air around areas of low pressure.

>> Out at sea, only the toughest ships can survive the huge waves whipped up by gales.

>> In a satellite photo, you can spot a gale from its comma-shaped clouds.

⌃ A gale stronger than 88 kilometres per hour can uproot trees and damage cars and buildings.

35

# Tornadoes

Tornadoes are like massive vacuum cleaners. They are powerful enough to suck up cars and houses.

<< When a tornado forms over water, it is called a waterspout.

Tornadoes are also called twisters. Their funnel-shaped clouds are easy to recognize. The spinning air in a tornado can reach 480 kilometres per hour.

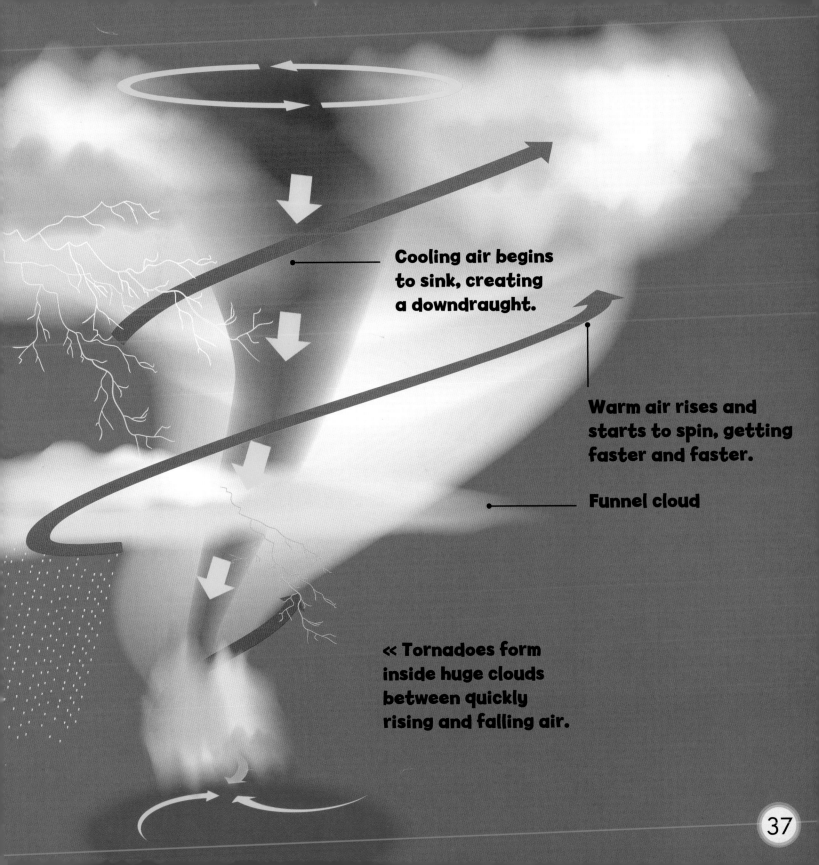

Cooling air begins to sink, creating a downdraught.

Warm air rises and starts to spin, getting faster and faster.

Funnel cloud

« Tornadoes form inside huge clouds between quickly rising and falling air.

# Hurricanes

**Hurricanes** are huge, spiralling storms. Inside a hurricane, the wind blows at more than 120 kilometres per hour.

« In Asia, hurricanes are called typhoons. In 2013, Typhoon Haiyan hit the Philippines, destroying a million homes.

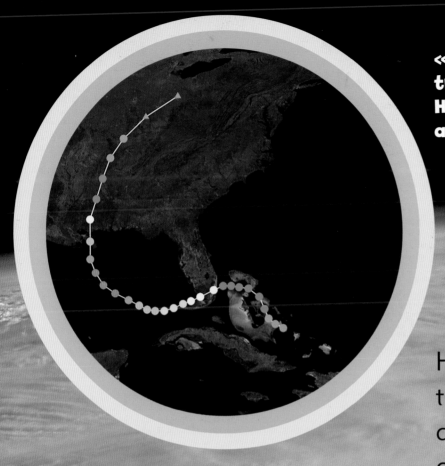

<< **A weather satellite tracks the course of Hurricane Katrina in 2005 across the Gulf of Mexico.**

Hurricanes form over tropical oceans. Hot, damp air rises quickly, creating high walls of cloud and heavy rain. The storm soon begins to spin around a calm centre, called an eye.

<< **This is Hurricane Isabel seen over Florida, USA, in 2003. Hurricanes are given names by weather forecasters.**

# Blizzards

A blizzard happens when fierce winds blow falling snowflakes or snow that has already settled on the ground.

>> In January 1996, a massive blizzard hit New York City. Up to 76 centimetres of snow fell in just two days.

<< If a blizzard stops you seeing more than a few metres ahead, it is called a 'whiteout'.

>> A blizzard leaves behind piles of snow called snowdrifts.

To be called a blizzard, a snowstorm has to have winds faster than 56 kilometres per hour. It also has to reduce visibility to less than 400 metres ahead.

# Sandstorms

Sandstorms and duststorms happen when winds blow huge clouds of sand or dust into the air.

« Sand and dust sting your eyes and fill your ears, nose and mouth.

In a sandy desert, strong winds can lift grains of sand and carry them for many kilometres. In dry, dusty areas, the same can happen with soil.

**˅ Sandstorms are often whipped up in the deserts of the Middle East.**

**>> Blown sand can rub away at rocks, sculpting them into strange shapes.**

# Droughts

A drought is when rain does not fall for weeks, months or even years. Droughts often happen in hot areas near the Equator.

˅ The Sahel region of Africa, close to the Sahara Desert, suffers droughts. The soil is baked and cracked.

« This woman is digging for drinking water at the bottom of a dried-up river in Kenya, Africa.

Without rain, crops and grass shrivel and die. Then the animals that feed on them starve. If all food supplies run out, people can become hungry and thirsty, too.

⩔When trees and plants dry out, just one spark can start a wildfire.

# Floods

When rivers overflow their banks or the sea washes far inland, it is called a flood.

Heavy rain can make rivers or lakes flood. In cities, rain sometimes falls so fast that the water cannot drain away through the concrete. Flood water can wash away cars and weak buildings.

« Fierce gales and hurricanes can cause storm surges. The sea level and waves rise high, flooding the coast.

>> When heavy rain falls on steep slopes, it can loosen the soil until there is a rockslide.

^ There is often flooding during Thailand's wet season, called the monsoon.

47

# Forecasting the weather

Everyone likes to know what the weather will do next. Some people, like farmers, depend on weather forecasts to earn a living.

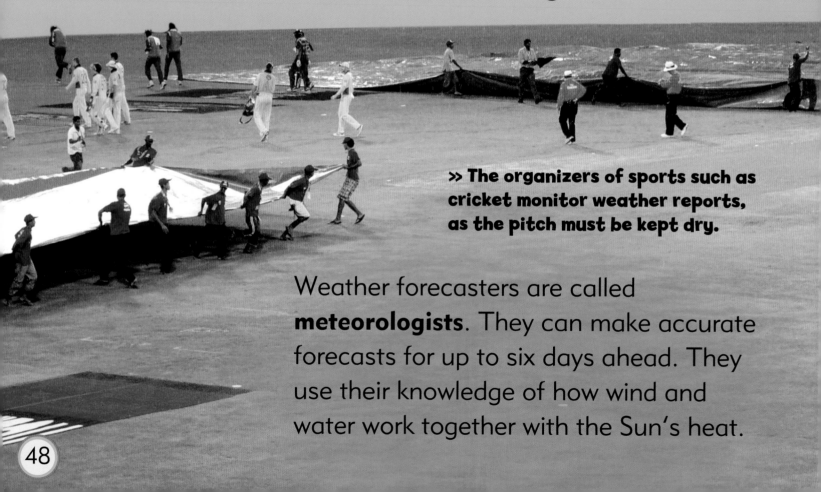

>> **The organizers of sports such as cricket monitor weather reports, as the pitch must be kept dry.**

Weather forecasters are called **meteorologists**. They can make accurate forecasts for up to six days ahead. They use their knowledge of how wind and water work together with the Sun's heat.

48

>> When snow is forecast, snow ploughs get ready to clear roads.

<< The forecast is often shown on a map, with symbols to represent areas of high pressure and low pressure.

H
1031

1000
1004

1028

# Weather stations

Across the world, there are thousands of weather stations. They collect information about the weather in their local area.

⌃ This is a weather buoy. It collects data about air and sea temperatures.

Forecasters need to know how the atmosphere is behaving all over the world. Weather stations collect information like temperature, wind speed, rainfall and cloud formations. Using computers, they share their reports around the world.

# Instruments

Weather stations use special instruments to take measurements. At home, you can measure rainfall, or check wind direction with a pocket compass.

**« An anemometer is an instrument that records wind speed and direction.**

**>> With a simple rain gauge placed in your garden, you can measure how much rain falls in a day.**

The simplest instrument is a rain gauge. More complicated instruments are barometers to measure **air pressure**, ceilometers for cloud height, and hygrometers to measure water vapour in the air.

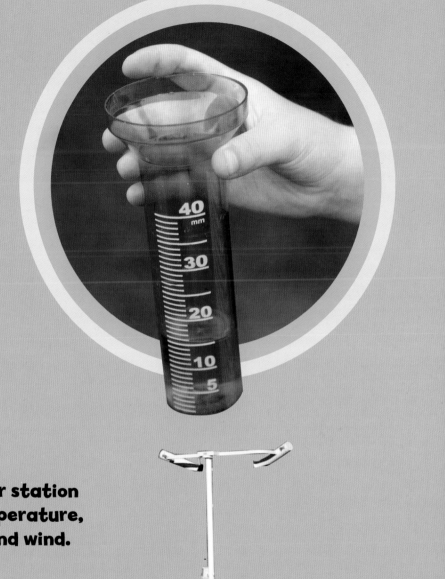

**⌄ This weather station measures temperature, air pressure and wind.**

# Weather balloons

Weather stations can only take measurements on the ground. To measure conditions high in the atmosphere, we need balloons.

Every day, about 2000 weather balloons are launched worldwide. Each carries instruments to measure temperature, wind speed and air pressure.

>> A balloon holds a package of instruments called a radiosonde. It sends information back to Earth by radio.

<< Balloons are usually filled with the gas hydrogen. It is lighter than air, so the balloons float.

<< Each radiosonde has a parachute to carry it gently to the ground when the balloon pops.

# Weather satellites

More than a dozen weather satellites are circling the Earth. They send down photographs of clouds, storms, snow and ice.

>> **Visible light photos show clouds. By studying these photos, forecasters can tell which way a storm is heading.**

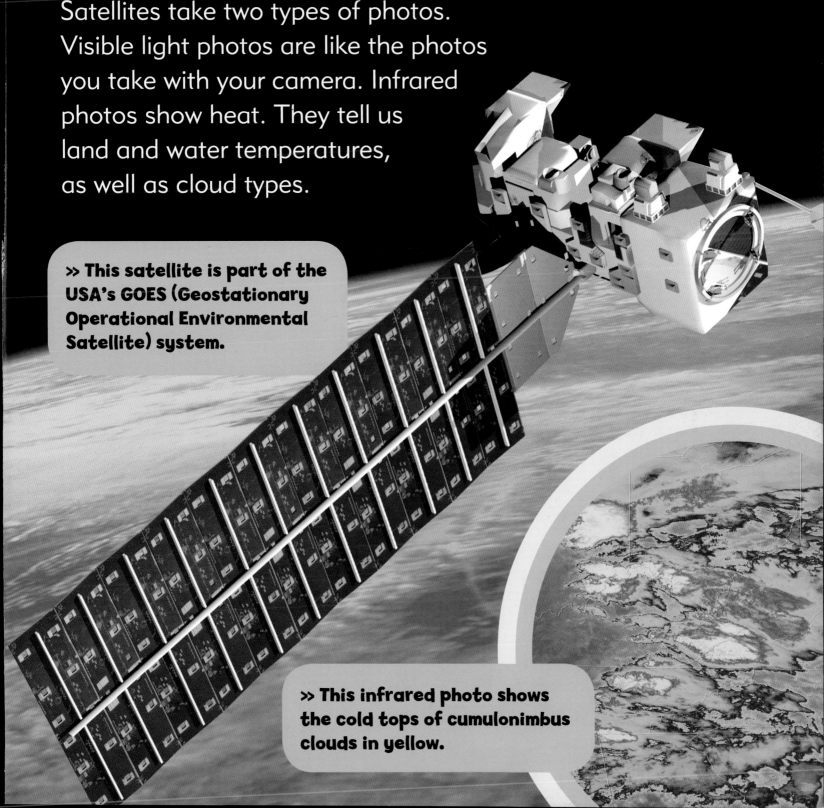

Satellites take two types of photos. Visible light photos are like the photos you take with your camera. Infrared photos show heat. They tell us land and water temperatures, as well as cloud types.

>> This satellite is part of the USA's GOES (Geostationary Operational Environmental Satellite) system.

>> This infrared photo shows the cold tops of cumulonimbus clouds in yellow.

# Supercomputers

Weather forecasters use supercomputers to predict the weather. These computers can make more than 1000 trillion calculations per second!

<< A supercomputer uses a model that divides the world into a grid. It works out the behaviour of air and water inside each square of the grid.

Many countries have a national weather service in charge of forecasting the weather. Each service collects information from stations, balloons and satellites, then feeds it into supercomputers.

⌃ Computers work out which way a hurricane is going. Then forecasters warn people.

« Supercomputers cost up to £100 million. They can usually give accurate forecasts for the next few days.

# Glossary

**air** The invisible gases that surround the Earth.

**air pressure** The force created by the weight of air pressing down on the Earth.

**atmosphere** The blanket of air that surrounds the Earth.

**climate** The weather conditions typically seen in an area over many years.

**condense** To change from a gas to a liquid.

**Equator** An imaginary line round the middle of the Earth.

**evaporate** To change from a liquid into a gas.

**forecaster** A person who uses instruments and computers to predict the weather.

**hurricane** A spiralling storm that forms over tropical oceans.

**ice crystal** Frozen water shaped into shapes such as snow flakes.

**low pressure** An area where warm air is rising. High pressure is caused by cool air falling.

**meteorologist** Person who studies the Earth's atmosphere.

**poles** The most northerly and southerly points on the Earth's surface.

**satellite** A device that circles far above the Earth to collect information or to send and receive signals.

**shockwaves** Movements of air that travel outward from a spark of lightning or an explosion.

**static electricity** An electric charge created when objects rub against each other.

**symmetrical** With sides or halves that mirror each other.

**temperate** A climate that is neither very hot nor very cold.

**temperature** A measure of heat and cold.

**tropical** A climate that is warm to hot all year.

**water vapour** Water that is in the form of a gas.

**weather** The state of the atmosphere at a particular place and time.

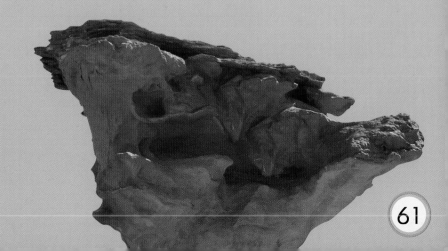

# Index

# Picture credits